Many Paths:
Reflections on a
Christian Journey

by Kara Wagner Sherer

MANY PATHS

Reflections on a Christian Journey

All Rights Reserved.

Copyright © 2014 By Kara Wagner Sherer

Cover illustration © Brad Gehrig

St. John's Episcopal Church

3857 N. Kostner Ave., Chicago IL 60641

ISBN:978-0-9888733-0-8

To the people of St. John's
especially Kathy Broderick,
who made this happen

Introduction

The idea for this little book of sermons came to me on a Sunday morning in August during one of St. John's "Gospel on the Green" services. In the beautiful, intimate garden, under the shade of a giant cottonwood tree, Kara Wagner Sherer preached about the mystery of the Eucharist. I don't know if it was the novelty of sitting outside for mass or her allusions to Harry Potter, but some niggling question inside of me was answered that day. Afterward, I casually said to Kara that she "should do a book."

I said this because Kara does not write out her sermons. Instead, she jots her notes on an index card, and then speaks extemporaneously. Unless a member of the congregation asks her to please commit the sermon to paper, Kara's exact words are lost to us. So, over the next year or so, in an attempt to capture her warm and playful style of preaching—and to collect the words of a woman who is not only a busy priest, but a wife and mother as well—I asked Kara to write down more of her sermons. Sermons that, to me, reflected her personality and made me very grateful to have come to church that day. (Her sermon on the Eucharist appears on page 58.)

The twenty-two sermons that follow are not printed in the order they were delivered. Rather, they flow together in a way that unfolds what I believe to be her simple and important message—that the Bible offers much meaning to the twenty-first century reader and that today's Christian community is vital and open to all those seeking to better the world. I hope the readers of this volume will enjoy Kara's sermons as much as I do. It is my hope that others may recognize her unbounded faith, great wisdom, and sense of humor. And if you'd like to hear Kara's very pleasant voice, you can access some audio files on the St. John's website (www.stjohnschicago.com).

In peace,
Kathy Broderick

Choose Your Own Ending

Genesis 6: 9-22; 7:24; 8:14-19
Matthew 7: 21-29

One day in a neighborhood just like ours, there was a sudden, freak flood. It started raining on Saturday night, and it rained for twenty-four hours straight. Then it stopped, and just as suddenly as it had come, all the water disappeared. When

Third Sunday after Pentecost

people came down out of their attics they looked around, and, miraculously, nothing appeared to be damaged. Their neighbors were all there, and none of their homes had been swept away. And then they looked down the street and saw an empty lot.

"Didn't there used to be something on the corner?" asked one neighbor.

"Yeah, I think there was a church there," said another.

"It was a pretty church. I walked by it in the mornings," said a third. "I never went in."

"How strange," thought all the neighbors.

But since nothing else seemed to have changed, they didn't give it another thought. What they didn't know was that about fifty people were in the church when the flood came. The whole church had turned upside down, the wooden roof became the bottom of the boat, and they just floated away.

They floated out of the city until they bumped up against St. Peter's Gate. Bang, bang, bang, went the boat on the gate, like knocking. But St. Peter didn't seem to be there. Finally they saw a man, off in the distance. He looked a bit suspicious of them, but finally someone recognized him.

"Jesus!" said one woman, "Jesus! Here we are—we're Christians. We've been doing your work for about 150 years, pledging, doing good deeds. And now we're here. See, we've even brought the church along so you could see it."

"Christians?" said Jesus. "I don't know that word. I'm sure you've done very important things, but I don't know you."

And he turned and walked away. The people didn't know what to do. They didn't know how to go home, and they couldn't get in the gate. So they sat in the boat, gently knocking against the gate, and told stories of how great things had been.

But this is a choose-your-own-ending sermon!

One day in a neighborhood just like ours, there was a sudden, freak flood. It started raining on Saturday night, and it rained for twenty-four hours straight. Then it stopped, and just as suddenly as it had come, all the water disappeared. When people came down out of their attics they looked around, and, miraculously nothing appeared to be damaged. But when they got out of their houses, they noticed some of their neighbors were missing.

"Where is Elbert? Where's Iris? Where's Susan? What happened to Ray?" they asked each other. Then they looked down the street and saw an empty lot. "Where is the church? They must have all been in the church when the flood was at its highest!"

Losing their neighbors was bad enough, but as they stood around the spot where the church had been, they realized what else they had lost.

"Where are we going to go for our AA meetings?" asked one woman.

"That was where I had Thanksgiving dinner the year my wife died, and I had nowhere to go," said one man.

"It's not only that," said another. "I remember the year they hired a bus, and we went down to the state capital to ask for health care reform. That was the year it finally happened."

"That church kept my family together," said another man. "My wife didn't have her papers, and they wrote letters to convince the INS to let us stay together."

"That church saved my life," said one young man, "I was in trouble in high school, and I went there for tutoring. My tutor is still my mentor."

What the neighbors didn't know was that all the people had been in the church on Sunday morning when the flood came. The whole church had turned upside down, the wooden roof became the bottom of the boat, and they just floated away. They floated along the streets until they bumped into a vacant lot about three miles west of their old neighborhood. They pried open one of the doors, and someone improvised a plank down to the ground. The people went out of the boat—in groups of twos, and threes, and fours. They looked around and saw that there were hungry people, and people who were suffering, and people in need.

"This looks just like home," they said.

And they got to work.

Jesus said, "Everyone then who hears these words of mine and acts on them will be like a wise man who built his house on rock. The rain fell, the floods came, and the winds blew and beat on that house, but it did not fall, because it had been founded on rock."

What kind of house are we building here, at St. John's?

What Makes a Place Holy?

Exodus 3:1-15

God said to Moses: Come no closer! Remove the sandals from your feet, for the place on which you are standing is holy ground.

Sixteenth Sunday after Pentecost

What makes a place holy? Is a place holy because a religious authority says that it is? Is a place holy because only holy things are done in it? Is a place holy because it is extraordinarily beautiful? Or ancient? What makes a place holy?

Last Sunday our family took the train into New York City, into Grand Central Station. Though it was Sunday morning, there were already hundreds of people on the streets. The neon signs were still flashing in Times Square, and the garbage from Saturday night was piled on the streets, some in bags and bins, some not. As we walked further, the smell of urine got stronger. There seemed to be a layer of grime, of August heat and humidity and dirt, on everything and everybody. We walked to Twenty-Eighth Street and Ninth Avenue, to the Church of the Holy Apostles, where John and I were members when we lived in New York. We were a half hour early (you can tell we aren't members!), and there was almost no one in the sanctuary. The tile floors were a warm red, and the walls were cream colored. It was cool, and quiet and very *clean*. It was a holy place.

What makes a place holy?

I asked my family what other places on our trip were holy. Carlisle, our younger daughter, said the Lincoln Memorial. It was a crowded place, but there was a hush as people looked at the carving of that great man, and read his words carved on the walls and thought about the turbulent times he lived in. Madeleine, our older daughter, said Ellis Island was holy. She could feel the souls of all the people who had walked up those steps, who came with their hopes and dreams. John remembered our walk through Clifton Gorge in Ohio, an ancient streambed cut by the glaciers. We parked in the hot parking lot and walked into the woods. As we walked down into the gorge, the temperature dropped ten degrees. You could see the play of light on the leaves and in the ripples on the water. It was a holy place.

What makes a place holy?

Moses was going about his daily job, taking care of the sheep. For some reason he went a little higher up on Mount Horeb that day, and he saw an amazing sight, a bush that was burning, but not consumed. He had to check it out. God said to Moses: Come no closer! Remove the sandals from your feet, for the place on which you are standing is holy ground.

Moses stood in awe and wonder. But God didn't tell Moses to stay and worship God, or build a church, or a monument, or erect a plaque. God told Moses to go! Leave the holy place and free the people who were in bondage in Egypt. And how would Moses know if this crazy idea was a good one? Someday, God said, you will return and worship me on this mountain.

What makes a place holy?

This weekend we remember the anniversary of the horrible destruction to New Orleans and the Gulf Coast by Hurricane Katrina. The pictures have been playing again in my mind's eye: the fierce winds, powerful water, the people crowded into the stadium, the floating bodies, and the rotting houses. I think that when we saw those images, we understood that New Orleans and the Gulf Coast were holy places, and those were holy people. We just didn't realize it until they were destroyed.

What makes a place holy?

Today we are invited to remove the shoes from our feet, to recognize that every place and every person is holy. As Christians we are invited to recognize the holy before it is destroyed, to show the world that every place we walk is holy.

The In-Between Place

Jeremiah 29:1, 4-7
Psalm 66:1-12
Luke 17:11-19

A teacher once told me to pay attention to where the stories about Jesus take place. I'd forgotten that advice until this week, when I noticed that Luke's gospel story about the healing of the ten lepers takes place in "the region between Samaria and Galilee." An in-between place is not a good place to be; it's no-man's-land. The places mentioned

Twentieth Sunday after Pentecost

are also significant. Samaria was a region where Jews had intermarried with local people and mixed religious traditions. They were considered unclean by other Jews. Samaria equals bad. Galilee, though a bit of a backwater, was where good, clean, hardworking Jews lived and worshipped the "right" way. Galilee equals good. The lepers are in the region in between because no one wants them, Samarians or Galileans.

The in-between place reminds me of the area between Hyde Park, where I once lived, and the South Shore neighborhood. Between these two nice Chicago neighborhoods, literally across the tracks, was a no-man's-land, a place you didn't go at night. It was dangerous.

The in-between place also reminds me of the time

between childhood and adulthood, the time of adolescence, when you are neither a kid, nor an adult. It is an awkward, difficult time. I thought about my growing up in that in-between place. I grew up without a TV in my house; I was the only one in my school that didn't have a television. Kids teased me because I didn't know what was going on in all the shows they watched. Someone decided that the reason my family didn't have a TV was that we were poor, so they teased me about that too. It didn't help matters that my parents drove the same car they had ordered on their wedding day, a 1967 AMC Rambler, blue, with what my father called "French lace" around the bottom. They were still driving that rusty car when I was in high school. It wouldn't have mattered if I told them that my Dad had paid cash for our house. We were poor, and I was made fun of because of it. I grew up knowing what it was like to be teased for something I had no control over. I can laugh about it now, but at the time it was very painful.

I survived. Others don't. This week we heard about five teenagers who committed suicide this month after being bullied. One was called a whore; four others were taunted because of their real or perceived sexual orientation. Adolescence is a dangerous, difficult place to be.

It is in this in-between place that Jesus heals the lepers. It is an unusual healing, almost by remote control. Out of respect, the lepers keep their distance from Jesus, not wanting to make him unclean, or to infect him. They cry out for help.

Jesus tells them to go and show themselves to their priests, which is how lepers were certified to be clean and could rejoin the community. And as they go, they are healed. That is why some of us go back to our hometowns, or to a high school reunion to show off. "See! I turned out o.k. despite what you said about me! Look at me, I am clean."

But not everyone can go home. The people of Israel, in our reading from Jeremiah, have gone from the safety of their homeland, through the in-between place as war refugees, into exile in a foreign land. There is little hope of ever returning. Jeremiah tells them to build houses, plant crops, marry, and have children. Bloom where you are planted. It gets better.[1]

Today we will pray for healing, lay hands, and anoint with oil. It is a recognition that we have all been to the in-between place; that some of us are in that difficult and dangerous place right now. We ask for prayers because we all desire wholeness in body, mind, and spirit. This Sunday's gospel reminds us that that is where Jesus comes to us—in the in-between places, in no-man's-land, in the dangerous places of our lives. There Jesus offers to heal us, reminds us, in the words of the psalm: "God holds our souls in life and will not allow our feet to slip."

---

1   It Gets Better refers to a series of videos on YouTube initiated by LGBT adults encouraging teenagers to persevere against bullies and make it through middle school and high school, because life gets better.

One Way to God

John 6:35, 41-51

I do not think that Jesus said the words we just heard
from the gospel of John. I say this out of historical knowledge.
Scholars tell us that the stories and sayings of Jesus were
passed down orally after his death and resurrection. After
a generation they began to be written
down. Mark was the earliest gospel,
and Luke and Matthew share most of
the same stories and sayings, though each seems to shape the
details and narrative to speak to their particular audience.

*Tenth Sunday
after Pentecost*

The Gospel of John is a whole other kettle of fish. Written
at least two generations after Jesus' death and resurrection,
it contains stories not found in any other gospel, stories told
in different order, and long speeches by Jesus—containing
passages like we read today—instead of short simple parables.
John was writing to Jewish Christians who were being
thrown out of the synagogues because of their belief in Jesus.
The author goes to great pains to show that Jesus predicted
their suffering, and that even the disciples had difficulty
understanding and believing what Jesus preached. The author
wanted to convince the reader that Jesus was the way to God.

I also do not *believe* that Jesus said the words we just
heard from the gospel of John. I say this from personal

conviction. I believe Jesus did everything he could to heal, restore, and save everyone he encountered, going out of his way to encounter people everyone else avoided. But this passage from John has been too easily manipulated to exclude people from Jesus' message. For example: "Your ancestors ate the manna in the wilderness, and they died," has been interpreted as claiming the Jews, and anyone before Jesus, had no access to salvation. The passage, "Very truly, I tell you, whoever believes has eternal life," has been interpreted to mean that the only way to God is through Jesus.

I remember wrestling with this question from a very early age. When I was about nine, I asked my dad what would happen to all the people in the world who had never heard of Jesus. He said he believed every person had some experience of God before they died. This wasn't a good enough answer for me. I can never believe that a God of love, who is desperate to restore all of creation, won't go to any lengths to provide a way to salvation for everyone, even those have who never heard of Jesus.

I was steeped in this theology—the one that says that only Jesus saves, and there is only one way to live this truth—when I attended the Leadership Summit at Willowcreek Church in Barrington this week. That church has a membership of seventeen thousand. The room seats six thousand. The set design, musicians, light show, and video interviews were of professional quality. The speakers were nationally and internationally known—from former British Prime Minister Tony Blair to Bono (who joined us via video)—and were leaders in business, academia, and religion. There is a lot that I, and all of us, can learn about not offering mediocre worship to God. But I couldn't let go of the underlying message that was being preached. I heard over and over that there is *one way* to God, and they knew the way to get there. I was also surrounded by hidden messages about what that way looked like. Of the seventeen speakers: eleven white men. I am not implying they didn't have good things to say, but that only left room for four men of color and two white women. I didn't hear a thing about what it means to be a woman of color leading in this world! Those who introduced the speakers took pains to tell us to whom the speaker was married and how many kids they had. It would have saved a lot of time if they just worn signs saying: I am not gay.

I believe that Jesus has been, and continues to be, my way to God. I came to know the good news of Jesus in the Episcopal Church. I believe I have experienced God, and continue to grow in the knowledge and love of God, and I expect to know the fullness of God's presence someday. I also think there are plenty of people who can find God through the message of Jesus preached here at St. John's. We can fill every pew and there would be more who would want to come in.

I also believe that people are finding God one block from here at the Baptist church. People are finding God at

St. Viator's Roman Catholic Church and at Mount Olive, an Evangelical Free Church. People are finding God at the Muslim Community Center on Elston, at the Buddhist Meditation Center on Montrose, and at the Emanuel Synagogue on Lake Shore Drive. Because our God so desperately wants to be found, there are opportunities to find God at the bar down the road, at the YMCA, at the Jewel, and yes, in the midst of six thousand people at Willowcreek Church.

What was the author of John trying to communicate when he has Jesus say, "No one can come to me unless drawn by the Father who sent me?" I hear that this is not about Jesus, but that only God provides the way, and if Jesus is the true way to God, then Jesus leads us back to God. Jesus is a conduit to God. "No one can come to me unless drawn by the Father who sent me." How do we know that Jesus is a true conduit to God? John says he is "living bread." If Jesus heals, restores, and feeds us—if Jesus leads us to God—then Jesus is a way to God.

How do I know that Osama Bin Laden is not a conduit to God? He is not living bread. How can you judge a way to God? By whether or not that way leads to God.

As a white, middle-class girl from small town Minnesota, I found God through the Jesus preached by the word and actions of the people in my little Episcopal church. The good news is that you don't have to be a white, middle-class girl from Marshall, Minnesota, to be saved!

The good news is that our God so desperately loves us, yearns for all of creation, that God provides a way for everyone, wherever you were born, whatever your culture or language. There is a way to God; there are many, many ways.

Animal Heaven

Isaiah 11:1-10

Perhaps it's just in my line of work, but I often find myself in meetings or seminars where we have to learn people's names in some creative new way. Most name games I don't mind, but I dread the moment when someone asks, "If you

Second Sunday of Advent

could be an animal, which one would you be?" I just have no idea. I'm not an animal person. I really like being human, and I can't imagine being an animal. Animals inhabit another world, one that I don't understand.

We were enjoying imagining another world during reflection group this week. We read the beautiful vision of Isaiah who imagines a time when, "The wolf shall live with the lamb, the leopard shall lie down with the kid, the calf and the lion and the fatling together, and a little child shall lead them." What a lovely vision. Muriel had seen a special on "Animal Planet" about a lion that was raising a gazelle as if it were her own cub, and Marilyn had seen the news about a leopard in Japan that had adopted some pigs. Isaiah's vision of the cow and the bear grazing together seemed almost possible. What a beautiful vision of a new kind of world!

We were wakened from our reverie by our seminarian, Jenny Jo, who has begun to cry "reality check" on a regular basis. "Why are we assuming that Isaiah is talking about animals?" she asked. "This is poetry, and it's full of metaphors, like the shoot of a tree growing out of a long-dead man named Jesse. Maybe this isn't about animals becoming herbivores, maybe this is about humans!"

Hmmm, that's an idea. We began to imagine what types of human beings are like wolves and leopards and lions and bears. (Oh my!) The over-functioners, type A, extroverted, strong. And who are like the lambs and calves and cows. The, unhurried, type B, introverted, take-life-as-it-comes folks. What if Isaiah was imagining all types of people living in harmony? What would that be like? Is that heaven?

I suspect the word heaven conjures up many different images for you. I propose three different visions of what heaven might be.

The first one I'll call High School Heaven. In this vision the perfect world works out just as high school was meant to be. In my high school the pressure was on to dress alike, to do the same things, to like the same things, to like the same people, to be the same. Hell was to stand out, to be different. Hell was to be rejected for your differences. So yes, Maddie, Heaven was to have Uggs, like everyone else. Everyone gets along because we are all the same. Is that your idea of heaven?

The second vision of heaven is the Holiday Party Heaven. You've probably already been to a holiday party. It's that time of year, and everyone gets together, whether you like each other or not. So families gather and try not to fight. And you probably have to gather with everyone from your work place. This would be my one chance to tell my husband's boss what I really think of him, only I can't because it's a holiday party! If only the cousins from Aurora would stay in Aurora, since they can only ever tell us how much better it is in Aurora. But no, it's the holidays, so they're coming! At holiday parties everyone gets together and pretends to like each other, pretends to agree, pretends to be having a jolly time...there is no conflict because it is all pretence. Is that your idea of heaven?

And then there is Isaiah's vision of heaven, where everyone is gathered, and everyone is different, but everyone is safe. In Isaiah's vision we are all different, but we can live together. We disagree, but we can walk with each other. We've hurt each other, but we've made amends, and now we can eat together. Men and women, teens and parents, over-functioners and under-functioners, type A and type B, gay and straight, extroverted and introverted, liberal and conservative. Even the toddler with chocolate smeared round her face dares to bury her head in Auntie's lap (the Aunt who doesn't like messy children). The secretary can be honest with the boss about his work and doesn't fear being fired.

But this isn't really heaven. This is what Isaiah, and what this season of Advent, is calling us to create in the here and now. This is the kingdom of God—a time when we recognize each other's differences, and acknowledge them, when we don't agree, but we still get along. This is the heaven we are called to create, here and now.

If I could be any animal, what would I be? I would be a human. I would be genuinely myself, and I wouldn't be afraid of standing out, or disagreeing. I wouldn't be afraid of any other human, however different. Strong or weak, we would all be safe because "they will not hurt or destroy on all God's holy mountain." This is the heaven we are called to create, here and now.

Ruby Bridges
A Palm Sunday Sermon

Isaiah 50:4-9a
Mark 14:1-15:47

Do you remember how that day began? Ruby Bridges really had no idea she would make history. She didn't know about Brown v. The Board of Education. She only knew that at the end of kindergarten she took a very difficult test with

Palm Sunday

hundreds of other black kindergarteners in New Orleans. She didn't know she was one of six girls to pass the test. She didn't know four girls would go to one school, one girl would remain in her old school, and she alone would integrate William Frantz Elementary. She didn't witness the visits from the NAACP members asking her parents to take the risk, to step out, for her sake and for the sake of African-American children all over. She learned all that later. On November 14, 1960, her mother just told her she was going to a new school, and she needed to behave. There might be a lot of people outside the school, but she didn't need to worry.

Do you remember how this day began? This day began with a trip to Jerusalem to celebrate the Passover. It could be dangerous. It was dangerous for everyone if the Romans were in the mood to make examples of the Jewish people, to show their power, to remind the victims that they were victims (as if they weren't reminded every day). But if you were a good Jew you went to Jerusalem for Passover, and so they went, Jesus and his friends.

What does it mean to believe in something, but to be unsure if you are right, or if it's the right time, or if you are the right person to be doing it?

Ruby got into the car with her mother and four federal marshals. She remembers thinking it was Mardi Gras, because there were so many people in the streets, and they were throwing things. She didn't really hear all the angry shouting of "Nigger go home" and "I will poison you." She did remember that one woman put a black baby doll in a coffin and held it up. That scared Ruby more than all the shouting. But her mother told her to say her prayers whenever she was scared. So she did. Ruby prayed for all the people shouting at her. Then she set her face and walked into her new school.

The Hebrew prophet Isaiah knew what it was like to stand for something unpopular:

"I gave my back to those who struck me, and my cheeks to those who pulled out the beard; I did not hide my face from insult and spitting. The Lord God helps me; therefore I have not been disgraced; therefore I have set my face like flint, and I know that I shall not be put to shame."

How? Where did that confidence come from?

Without thinking about it, Ruby knew her parents loved her and would never want her to be hurt. She was too young to question their judgment. So she went to school every day and sat in a classroom, by herself, with the only white teacher who agreed to teach her. She never went to recess or the lunchroom.

We know from the stories that Jesus took time to pray, went off by himself. He knew God loved him, deeply, passionately. He knew God wanted him to be truly himself, never to waver from the life God was calling him to lead. He knew he was to love the unpopular people, speak the unpopular truth. God would never want him to be hurt, but whatever the consequences, God would see him through.

Maybe the edgy political demonstration, riding into Jerusalem on a donkey like the ancient kings of Israel, deliberately provoking the Roman rulers, was the wrong choice. But he loved these people, he wanted them to be free. He had chosen this road. God's love kept moving him forward even when the shouts of praise turned to "Crucify him!" Even when his friends deserted him in fear.

Do you know God's love so deeply? So truly? Are you willing to depend on that love at any cost?

Can we pray this prayer today? "Jesus, when you rode into Jerusalem, the people waved palms with shouts of acclamation. Grant that when the shouting dies we may still walk beside you even to a cross."

Jesus Walked into High School

Proverbs 1:20-33
Mark 8:27-38

Jesus walked into high school on the first day. He was with Peter and James. They hadn't gone to elementary school with him, but they went to the same synagogue, and they'd been friends since they could remember.

Fifteenth Sunday after Pentecost

Jesus looked around at the kids streaming in and asked his friends, "Who do people say I am?"

James said, "Some people say you're a jock, some say you are a nerd, and some people think you are a goody-goody, acting good just to get the teachers on your side."

Jesus asked them, "But who do you think I am?"

Peter said, "You are my best friend, the best friend anyone could have."

They shut up fast when they saw a group of kids coming towards them; they didn't want anyone to hear what they were saying. Jesus gave Peter a push, and James started doing jump shots near the lockers. The first day had begun.

But it was a month later, sitting in the cafeteria, when Jesus really began to say weird things. Peter was talking about how lucky Jesus was to have so many friends. It seemed like anyone would talk to him.

"It isn't going to last," Jesus said. "As soon as they get to know me, it'll change. If I really want to be myself—live my life the way I want to—the jocks will hate me, the nerds will call me a reject, and the goody-goodies will pretend I don't exist. They'll slam me against the lockers and humiliate me. But I have to do it. I have to be who I am, no matter what they all think."

"Are you crazy?" whispered Peter. "Do you know what it means to be popular? This is your chance, and mine and James's too. Once you are in the Out crowd, you never get back In. Don't screw this up. If you go down, you take us all down."

Jesus looked at him, hard. He almost never got angry, but when he did, watch out! "I thought you were my best friend!" he said. "Don't you know what really counts? If you want to be my friend, you have to give up trying to fit in, making yourself into something you are not. If you would give anything to be in the In crowd, you'll end up on the bottom with nothing. What is the point of being popular if you forget who you really are?"

Jesus's voice suddenly stood out in the noisy room, and people were turning to look at them. James started dribbling a basketball, and Peter looked out the window. This was going to be a difficult year....

How rare it is to meet someone who is so comfortable in their own skin that they never judge you in yours. Jesus must have been such a person—wise. Wisdom has nothing to do with book learning or age. Wisdom only comes through life, a training forced on us. Though as we heard in the reading from Proverbs, not everyone chooses to pursue it.

We couldn't escape this fact on Wednesday during our reflection group. It is pretty clear that when Jesus says "take up your cross and follow me," he doesn't mean become an acolyte and carry a cross in church. We talked about people who had lost their lives for others. The usual names came up—Martin Luther King, Gandhi, Mother Theresa. But what about those closer to our circumstances?

This week our church marked the day an Episcopal nun named Constance died in 1878 in Memphis, Tennessee, of the yellow fever. That didn't make her a saint; almost five thousand people died in that epidemic. And she isn't a saint because she became a nun. No, she and her companions, sisters and priests, are remembered because they stayed in Memphis to care for the sick, those too poor to flee the city. They gave their lives serving others. They lost their lives for the sake of the gospel.

"For what shall it profit a man, if he shall gain the whole world, and lose his own soul?"

I wonder if Jesus was afraid to be who he really was, and face the hatred. I am afraid. I am afraid to take seriously the

Christian idea that following Christ means changing your life, and changing the world. But what if it's true? What if I have to be who I really am no matter what other people think?

In the King James translation of Mark's gospel, Jesus rebukes Peter saying, "for thou savourest not the things that be of God, but the things that be of men." What does it mean to "savourest the things of God"? To savor something is to taste it, enjoy it, and slowly discover its richness. Is that the cross that Jesus offers to us? A life to savor? Will savoring the things of God save our soul? How can that be something to be afraid of?

Savor your soul. It is a gift from God, and it is the only one you have.

Imprisoned and Freed

Acts 16:16-34

The Acts of the Apostles is my new favorite book of the Bible. Besides the Psalms, it seems to be the most relevant to our daily lives. The book of Acts tells the stories of the early Christians, figuring out what it meant to be Christians without

Seventh Sunday of Easter

Jesus around. Plus, Acts just has some great stories, like the one we heard today about Paul and Silas and the slave girl with the "power of divination."

There is a lot packed into this story, and every character reveals a different relationship with freedom and imprisonment. All the characters are imprisoned, and each responds to freedom differently.

The slave girl is chained to her owners, dependent on them for her livelihood. Yet she displays a kind of freedom as she follows Paul and Silas around, shouting the truth at them, "You are men of God." It would be as if a shrimp fisherman from Louisiana found the address of a BP executive and began to follow her around, not making any demands, but just shouting, "You have the power; you are in charge!"

The slave girl's freedom caused a ruckus in our reflection group this week. It was quickly pointed out that it was all well and good for Paul and Silas to free her...but for what?

How would she now support herself? We drew the parallel to the time after the Emancipation Proclamation when slaves were promised their freedom, forty acres, and a mule. They received their freedom, but never saw the forty acres or the mule. It is a good reminder to us who like to do good about how much responsibility we have for the lives we affect.

The slave girl's owners are prisoners, too—slaves to their own evil deeds. Once she is freed from her powers, they have no way to make a living. When she loses her powers, so do they. They remind us of drug lords of today.

Paul and Silas are literally imprisoned, shackled and locked up in a "maximum security cell" as *The Message* translates it. Yet they don't behave at all like people in chains. They sing and praise God. They behave as free people, proclaiming that truth will win in the end. Their story is echoed in the lives of those imprisoned for civil disobedience, singing "We shall overcome."

The jailer is imprisoned by his own job. Believing the prisoners to have escaped, he can only think of suicide. Just this week, we learned of the suicide of Phil Pagano, the Metra executive who was imprisoned by his own job. Faced with the revelations of stealing from the company, he threw himself in front of a train—dying by the very thing that imprisoned him.

You may have already forgotten the other prisoners in the jail; they are almost subtext. We can understand why Paul and Silas didn't run when the earthquake destroyed their chains and locks. They had a point to prove. But what about the other prisoners? They are suddenly faced with freedom, but are paralyzed. I am reminded of a friend who had a beagle. The dog behaved very badly at night, tearing the house apart. In desperation she finally decided to put the dog on a leash at night, and put the end of the leash under the leg of a chair. This worked very well. After about a month, she came down one night to discover that she hadn't secured the end of the leash under the chair. But it didn't matter. The dog hadn't moved. It believed that it was chained, and that was all that was needed. My friend never had to put the leash under the chair again.

What imprisons you? What do you need release from? What would you do with your freedom?

This past week we celebrated the Feast of the Ascension—the day we remember that after his death and resurrection and appearances to the faithful, Jesus was taken bodily into heaven. It is a strange concept, but perhaps this story from Acts helps us to understand the Ascension.

In celebrating the Ascension we claim that Jesus was a prisoner to nothing earthly. He belonged to God and returned to God.

Jesus was not held captive by popular opinion, not even on the day of his triumphal entry into Jerusalem on Palm Sunday. Jesus was not captive to human authority, even during his trial before the Romans. Jesus was not captive to suffering or even death. Nothing can hold him here, for he belongs only to God.

What imprisons you? What do you need release from? What would you do with your freedom?

Isaiah Inspired

Isaiah 61:1-4,8-11

Advent

I feel inspired to tell you—
I can't keep it in!
There is good news for the unemployed.
There is hope for broken families.
If you are bankrupt, be debt free.
If you've defaulted on your mortgage,
Come back home.
This is your lucky day.
With God, what goes around comes around.
God dries the tears of all who cry in pain.

I have gifts for anyone who is down.
A bouquet of flowers instead of bills,
A cup of joy instead of tears,
A coat of self-confidence instead of fear.
You are God's diamonds,
Forever catching the Light.

You will turn the neighborhood around,
Clean up the vacant lots,

Restore old homes to their former glory,
Open new shops in abandoned buildings.

For God loves justice,
Hates bribery and pay to play.
God will give you what you deserve.
This is a promise that will never be broken.

Your grandchildren will be famous all over the world,
Their children honored by everyone.
All who see them will know
That they are blessed by God.

I will shout at the top of my lungs,
And dance in front of everyone!
I'm wearing God's designer clothes—
I'm dressed to the nines in perfection and peace,
Like a groom in his expensive tuxedo,
Like a bride putting on her pearls.
Just like the dirt that suddenly turns to grass,
Like the garden that bursts into color in spring,
So God will make things right again.
It will happen before your very eyes.

Sheep

Acts 2:42-47

Last week a sixteen-year-old girl from the Yearning
for Zion Ranch in Texas called the child abuse hotline.
Law enforcement officers went to the ranch, a branch of the
Fundamentalist Church of Jesus Christ of Latter-Day Saints,

*Fourth Sunday
of Easter*

which practices polygamy. They knocked
on doors and interviewed members.
Finally they asked for a key to the
temple. Members politely refused, not wanting their place of
worship desecrated. So the chief called in a locksmith, who
was unable to move the dead bolts. They tried the "Jaws of
Life," which are normally used to open car doors after an
accident. These too failed. Finally they called in a SWAT team
to use brutal force. Fifty seven male members of the church
stood in a circle around the temple to "bear witness." As the
doors were broken down, some knelt in prayer, and others
sobbed. One man tried to intervene.[2]

Jesus says, "anyone who does not enter the sheepfold by
the gate but climbs in by another way is a thief and a bandit.
The one who enters by the gate is the shepherd of the sheep.
The gatekeeper opens the gate for him, and the sheep hear his

2   Johnson, Kirk, and Gretel C. Kovach, Officials Tell How Sect in West Texas Was
Raided: The New York Times; April 11, 2008.

voice. He calls his own sheep by name and leads them out. When he has brought out all his own, he goes ahead of them, and the sheep follow him because they know his voice."

Evidence found in the temple and conversations with members prompted officers to remove over four hundred children; mothers went with the children voluntarily. To those of us on the outside, the officers are saviors, bursting into an abusive and manipulative sect to free innocent children. But imagine if you had lived your whole life inside that compound, being told that the world outside the walls was evil. Even if you had some inkling that what was being done to you, or what you were told to do to others was wrong, the raid must have felt like an enormous violation. The pictures of the women show fear on their faces, not freedom.

We talk a lot about boundaries: "He has no boundaries," or "She got in my personal space," or "That crossed the line." But boundaries are elusive, because they are so personal, so individual. What one person perceives as crossing a line, another person might perceive as warm and friendly. What seems like a simple question to you may feel like an invasion of privacy to another.

I think Jesus' parable of the sheepfold is about boundaries. To get a glimpse of what Jesus is talking about we need to know a little bit about first-century Middle Eastern farming practices. The sheepfold is a communal sheep pen, a large fenced in area to which several shepherds bring their flocks at night. A gatekeeper is hired to watch the fence and keep out thieves and wild animals. In the morning the shepherds go to the sheepfold, the gatekeeper lets them in and they call to their sheep. The sheep know the voice of their shepherd and follow him out into the world, for the day's grazing.

As is often the case, Jesus states the obvious. The person who climbs over the fence is a thief. The person who observes boundaries is the one to be trusted. Jesus is reminding us to trust our instincts. You know when someone has violated your boundaries. You know who is a thief, and who is to be trusted. You know the voices you can trust.

But the disciples don't understand, and we are not so sure. Especially if, like the members of the Yearning for Zion Ranch, we have allowed another person to control our boundaries, if we've given over our freedom of choice to a set of religious rules that do not allow for questioning or doubt. How can we trust our instincts?

Jesus says, "I am the gate. Whoever enters by me will be saved, and will come in and go out and find pasture."

So Jesus offers an invitation, and it's as if he's saying: Look! I'll be your gate! I'll help you keep your boundaries. I'll remind you to trust your instincts. I'll point out the thieves. I'll help you recognize the voice of those you can trust. I am the gate. I come that you may have life, and have it abundantly.

There is a difference between the techniques of European

shepherds and Middle Eastern shepherds, even to this day. European shepherds get behind the sheep, prodding them with a staff, pushing them forward. Middle Eastern shepherds walk out in front of their sheep, calling to them, leading them to good pastures, and trusting that the sheep know their voice and will follow.

This church should not be a compound, walling you off from the world, dictating your life, taking away your choices. This church is a sheepfold, a place of rest and protection, a place where you can see over the fence, look over your life for an hour, renew your trust in your instincts, ask for God's guidance, and then go out, following the one whose voice you know, who calls you by name and guides you in grace and love.

The Death of Certainty

Mark 16:1-8

There is a Bible story that we don't hear very often. I'm not even sure we ever read it in church, but it is one of those stories that I remember distinctly from a childhood storybook. It is the story of Gideon, a man who believed he was being

------

Easter Sunday

called by God, but wasn't sure. The story is that he tested God. He said, "Okay God, I'm going to put this sheep's fleece out tonight. If in the morning the ground is perfectly dry, but the fleece is soaking wet, then I'll know it's really you." So he put the fleece out, and in the morning the ground was perfectly dry and the fleece was soaking wet, so wet he rung out a bowl of water from the fleece. But this wasn't enough for Gideon, who was a skeptic. "Okay God," he said, "that could have been a freak of nature. Tonight I'll put the fleece out again. This time, if the ground is wet with dew, but the fleece is perfectly dry, then I'll know it's really you." So he put the fleece out, and low and behold the next morning the ground was soaked with dew but the fleece was perfectly dry.

I think for many of us Easter morning is like the Gideon fleece test. We get all dressed up, plan a fancy dinner, invite our family and friends, drag them to church and say, "Okay God, if you are really out there, alive and working in my life, prove it! Let there be some story that is told, some piece of music that touches the soul, some concrete proof that you are alive."

And here we are. You all look good! The church looks beautiful. We are ready for some sign! And then we here the gospel story, the "proof" of Jesus' resurrection, but it isn't what we expected. The three women go to the tomb and find the stone is rolled away and Jesus' body isn't there. And a man dressed in white says, "he has risen"? And they are to tell the other disciples that Jesus will meet them in Galilee. They are so shocked...they are filled with terror and amazement and "*they say nothing to anyone* because they are afraid." Terror, amazement, and fear. How's that for an Easter sermon? How's that for proof? We wanted certainty!

But is that really what we are here for? Do we really want certainty? Religious certainty has not served us well in the past. Scripture suggests that it was religious certainty that prompted the religious leaders of Jesus' time to hand him over to be crucified. Religious certainty got us witch burnings in the European Middle Ages. Religious certainty impels polygamous ranches to be built in the United States, and whole families to be shut away from the world. Religious certainty brought us the terrors of September 11.

I was afraid to preach the death of certainty, to preach terror, amazement, and fear. But if this gospel suggests any theme to me it is the death of certainty. We say that the only thing sure is death and taxes, and April 15 is three days away, so that's pretty certain! But the story of Jesus' resurrection tears away at the notion that even death is certain, final. Jesus breaks open the gates of hell; the laws of nature are turned upside down. What is certain?

Yet I also did not want to stand before you today and declare, "Nothing is certain but that there is no certainty!" That's just intellectual fiddle-faddle, and besides I don't believe it. I had to ask myself, I can't be certain of the virgin birth, or the bodily resurrection of Jesus, or the ascension, what can I be certain of?

I know in my own life, when I've encountered terror, or amazement, or fear, I have also known love. I know I am loved, that there is love so abundant that I can't soak it all up, and there is plenty left for every other person in the world. I am pretty sure about love.

It is love that makes it possible to stand before you today and say that if you have lost your job, you may find a better one, and you will find new life. Love also makes it possible for me to say that if you have lost your job, you may lose your house; you may have to declare bankruptcy. But at the bottom of the financial ruin, Love will be there.

Love makes it possible for me to say that if you have a broken marriage, it is possible to find forgiveness and healing, and your marriage will become new. But it is possible that healing will come through divorce and separation, and that at the bottom of that pain Love will be there to see you through.

Love makes it possible for me to say that if you have cancer, they may find a cure, and you will live many healthy years. But love also makes it possible to say that there may not be a cure, you may face death, and Love will carry you through. Death is not the final answer; there is new life.

We are here to celebrate the death of certainty, to celebrate that if we are able to admit to our terror, look with amazement, and face our fears, if we are willing to cut the safety net of certainty, we will drop into the arms of Love. Of this I am sure.

Birth and Death

Ephesians 1:11-23
Luke 6:20-31

Today is our second daughter Carlisle's birthday. She was
born early in the morning on a Sunday, the day our church
celebrated the Feast of All Saints. I wasn't working in the
church then, and John missed playing for the services. But

All Saints Day

after all the excitement died down, at
about one in the afternoon, John asked
sheepishly, "If it's okay with you, I think I'll go and conduct
the concert." Fourth Presbyterian has a tradition of having
the choir sing a requiem for an evening service on All Saints
Sunday. That night he conducted the John Rutter Requiem.
Tonight he'll conduct the Fauré Requiem. It might seem
strange to some people that John would witness his daughter's
birth in the morning and conduct music for a funeral mass in
the afternoon.

We have another such juxtaposition today. This morning
we will celebrate Anna's baptism—she will be the newest
Christian in our community. We will make promises, splash
water, and joyfully welcome her. Then a few minutes later we
will read the names of those who have died in the past year,
remembering our loved ones by lighting candles in their honor.
Birth and death. It is a lot to do in one day, one hour.

But these strange coincidences are a good introduction to the Christian life. They are a reminder that living the way Jesus called us to live is radically different from the way the world asks us to live. And there is no better passage from scripture to remind us of this than the one we just heard, the Beatitudes from Luke, or as a seminarian might call it, "the really long speech by Jesus in the middle of the gospel": Congratulations if you are poor! Congratulations if you are hungry! Congratulations if you are crying right now! That's what it says…and then it gets harsher: A curse on you who are rich! A curse on you if you are full! A curse on you who are laughing now, for you will mourn and weep.

Jesus is telling us to watch out—the world is about to be turned upside down. And then Jesus gives one paragraph of clear and simple instructions on how that will happen. "But I say to you that listen, Love your enemies…" Thanks, Jesus, for starting out easy! *Enemies.* That doesn't mean your friends and family and the people who irritate you. He means love the people who deliberately work to hurt and destroy you. "Do good to those who hate you," (well, that might mean your family!). "Bless those who curse you, pray for those who abuse you."

And in case you think Jesus is telling us to be doormats and let the world walk all over us, listen to the next line. "If anyone strikes you on the cheek, offer the other also." That isn't about a victim who has been beaten down, that is about someone who has the ability to strike back, who wants to hit back, but has the strength and courage to clench her fist at her side. It is a call for nonviolent resistance.

"From anyone who takes away your coat do not withhold even your shirt." My friend Bridget says this is comic relief, after all these difficult instructions. If someone took your coat and you gave them your shirt you'd be practically naked! It is a way to embarrass your attacker.

"Give to everyone who begs from you." Now this I have a hard time with. I promised myself never to give money to a beggar. Instead, I give a smile, some food, or a Hands to Help card and encourage them to come to St. John's on Wednesday to get some real help. Jesus says, "Give to everyone who begs from you."

In preparing for today's baptism, Sara told me a story that happened when they first moved into their neighborhood. They were getting gas at the station where Peter always filled up the car. There was a homeless man sitting on the curb when they pulled up. Peter ran over to him, "Hi John, I want you to meet my wife Sara!" He was introducing her as if he was at a cocktail party for work. Sara said she is a little worried about the time Peter will take Anna to meet the local homeless guy. But she shouldn't be worried. Peter is just teaching Anna to keep her baptismal promises, to treat all people with dignity and respect, no matter who they are.

These are the riches of our inheritance, as Paul calls them

in his letter to the Ephesians. These promises are the keys to turning the world upside down. Today we will renew our promise to live a Christian life. And then we will remember the people in our lives who have shown us one way to live a Christian life. As you light a candle, think of it as a gift for Anna; the life of your loved one shining in your life, and now in hers, shining as an example of Christian living.

Birth and death. Blessings and curses – a light in the darkness turning the world upside down. This is the richness of our inheritance.

Grief

Wisdom of Solomon 3:1-9
Psalm 24
Revelation 21:1-6a
John 11:32-44

St. Gregory of Nyssa Episcopal Church, in San Francisco, is an Episcopal church that has embraced Orthodox traditions more than most. Members of the congregation listen to the Word facing one another in one part of the church and then

All Saints Day

literally dance (a simple walking and hopping dance) into the other part of the church, forming a circle around the altar, where they celebrate Communion. Above them on the ceiling is an icon called *The Dancing Saints*, depicting ninety full-sized saints, from traditional ones such as St. Teresa of Avila and St. Francis, to non-Christian people from all cultures, such as Malcolm X, Anne Frank, and Margaret Mead. My favorite is Elizabeth I, dressed in full regalia (a bit like the cope I'm wearing today!) and dancing not four figures down from Mahatma Gandhi in his simple white kurta. The icon is meant to remind the earthly worshippers that they are surrounded by this great cloud of witnesses dancing before the throne of God. I can't think of a better icon, or window, into the meaning of All

Saints Day than that icon of the dancing saints.[3]

But while All Saints Day is meant to be a great celebration, the readings today are all about grief. The first reading from the Wisdom of Solomon, with the comforting reminder that "the souls of the righteous are in the hand of God," is usually read at funerals. The reading from Revelation is also comforting, proclaiming that "the home of God is among mortals" and that God will come to "wipe every tear" from our eyes. So it is no accident that when the Wednesday reflection group met to read the story of Lazarus, we talked about death and grief.

The story of the raising of Lazarus is a unique one, found only in the Gospel of John. Jesus appears so human in this story. Jesus was told, you know, that Lazarus was sick. But Jesus didn't hurry back. When he finally arrived, Lazarus had been dead four days. Yet Lazarus was a good friend; Jesus had often dined in his home with him and his sisters, Mary and Martha. They had supported Jesus' ministry. As you read, you can feel Jesus' sense of guilt at not being present at Lazarus's last moments. And then Mary cries out to him, "Lord, if you had been here, my brother would not have died!" How many times have I heard that universal human cry: God if you really existed, this would not have happened.

What I noticed for the first time is that Jesus does not

3   To learn more about St. Gregory of Nyssa go to www.saintgregorys.org

grieve at the news of the death of Lazarus, but at the grief of Mary and Lazarus's friends. It is their pain that moves Jesus to tears. It is not for Lazarus that Jesus cries, but for Mary. This is true compassion, isn't it? Compassion means to "feel with" another person. As Walter said on Wednesday, "When I go to the funeral of a friend, I am fine until the wife and kids begin to cry. And then I lose it." It can be so painful to feel the suffering of others.

So I thought all week that these readings are meant to remind us that God is with us in our suffering, that God has compassion, that Jesus came to Earth to experience human suffering. But if this is so, why is it that at times of death God seems most absent? Why is it that anger at God is the most natural and common reaction to death? Why is it that we want to remember the good times and happy memories, but we can feel only grief and pain?

While we know in our heads that God is with us in grief, perhaps what this story really teaches is that grief makes us more like God. Grief makes us God-like. When we grieve, we forget about ourselves, our selfish desires, and have compassion for others—we "feel with" others. That is who God is, the one who is always compassionate, who always feels with us.

There are more dead people here today than there are living people. We will read the names of all those we loved who died in the past year, and there are pages more of all those we remember today. We will light candles on the altar in their memory. I hope you can imagine a great dance, as the smoke from the candles rises—our memories, the souls of our loved ones rising to dance, a great cloud of witnesses surrounding us, a bridge between earth and heaven. This is not an image made up to comfort us, but an expression of the reality that the souls never leave us, nor we them, and we too will join them in that great dance of the saints in eternity.

Pray Without Ceasing

Luke 18:1-8

When my girls were small, we started a way of praying that was a review of their day and their emotions. It started: "Dear God, today I felt happy (sad, mad, powerful, scared, peaceful) when.…"

Preached on October 17, 2010

Madeleine loved to pray this way. She usually had more than one story to tell for each emotion. Carlisle was younger and found it harder to think of how she had felt each day. One night, when Carlisle was about four, I sat down on her bed to pray.

"Mom," she said, "can we pray this way?" She got out of bed, knelt down, crossed herself, pressed her palms together, and closed her eyes.

I knew our two girls were different, but this reminded me … they are very different! And so is everyone, when it comes to what prayer works for us.

People often ask me to pray (something about the career I chose, I guess). Sometimes I feel a fraud. I think people imagine that once a day I put on a long white robe, come into the church, light candles, kneel on the hard, wood floor and pray for a couple of hours. If you believe that, I'll tell you which numbers to play on your next lottery ticket for the simple price of $1,000! Remember when I was doing twenty minutes of silence a day? Well, even that fell by the wayside.

Today we heard, "Jesus told his disciples a parable about their need to pray always and not to lose heart." Have you noticed this about Jesus? The Hebrew Scriptures require that a person give ten percent of their income, or potatoes, or time to the Lord. Jesus says, "sell all your possessions and give the money to the poor." The Hebrew Scriptures suggest that righteous people pray five times a day. Jesus says, "pray without ceasing." Thanks for upping the ante, Jesus!

Do you pray all the time? When someone asks me to pray, it means they are put into the Sunday bulletin, and their name is read aloud by the whole community. If a person is on the long-term prayer list they are prayed for every Wednesday. My praying for someone might mean giving them a call, thinking about them, or checking in with friends or family.

How do you pray? Some of you take the bulletin home and use it in your own private prayer. I don't spend hours on my knees, but someone else at St. John's does. Some people make casseroles and deliver them. Some people call or visit, or write a card. Sometimes giving a ride, or talking about a situation with other friends is a prayer. If I read a poem that reminds me of you, I send it. I had a good friend who cut out newspaper articles and pictures and sent them to me. I always felt held in his prayers.

And what is prayer? Is it sitting by someone's side in a

hospital bed, holding their hand? Is it a kiss or a hug? Is it shouting, "Help!" or "Oh shit!" or "Oh my God, I can't do it anymore."?" Is it going back to bed to cry? Digging a hole or washing the car or running around the block? Sitting up all night with a crying baby? What is prayer?

When I first read today's gospel, the story of the persistent widow as it is called, I thought I would preach about justice, because clearly that is what it is about. She cries out, and finally she gets what she deserves. Why? Because even though the judge has no fear of God and no respect for anyone, the widow irritates him enough so that he relents and gives her justice, for his own selfish reason.

But God is not like the unjust judge. We heard last week in the letter to Timothy (Timothy 2:8-15) that even if we lose faith, God must remain faithful, because God cannot deny God's self. God fears God, and has respect for all people, even the worst of us. So Jesus says, "Will not God grant justice to his chosen ones who cry to him day and night? Will he delay long in helping them?"

That's reassuring, and just what we want to hear. God will quickly hear our prayers and grant justice. Perfect end to the story; neatly tied with a bow.

Except it isn't the end. Jesus has one more question, "will he find faith on earth?" In other words, is anyone taking this promise seriously? Is anyone crying out to God? Do you pray without ceasing?

Scream, cry, fold your hands, get off your butt, pray, wherever and whenever. Because if you don't, how will God ever hear you?

Eating Flesh

John 6: 56-69

This week my oldest daughter was a junior counselor for Vacation Bible School at Fourth Presbyterian Church. At dinner she would tell us the highlights of the day, which seemed to be the snack.

Twelfth Sunday after Pentecost

The first day they had an assortment of marshmallows, raisins, gummy frogs—ten things that corresponded to the ten plagues of the Egyptians. But what really got Madeleine was the snack on the day they read the story of the Passover. Remember, Moses tells the Israelites to slaughter a lamb and daub the blood on the doorposts of their homes so that the Angel of Death passes over them. They were to eat the lamb and prepare bread without yeast, so that they would be able to leave at a moment's notice and escape from slavery in Egypt.

On that day at Vacation Bible School, the snack was a Ritz cracker with pizza sauce and shredded mozzarella cheese. The teachers told the kids that the cracker represented the unleavened bread, the pizza sauce was the blood, and the cheese pieces were the sticks used to daub the blood.

"These are kids!" Madeleine was indignant. "They kept asking us if they were eating blood!"

All I can say is that this is why I would never use a canned curriculum for Vacation Bible School. You need to check it out first. But I can't criticize the Presbyterians too much. You may have noticed that I've been avoiding talking about eating flesh and drinking blood lately. We've already had two Sundays from the gospel of John, and now this week the author has Jesus saying, "Unless you eat my flesh and drink my blood you cannot abide in me." What can this possibly mean? We aren't meant to take this literally are we? Of course, we are not the first Christians to be disturbed and confused by these words. We've been trying to figure this out for nearly 2,000 years.

Mostly we have tried to explain these words through our theology of the Eucharist—communion, what the bread and the wine mean. For the first 1,500 years or so the primary explanation of communion has been *transubstantiation*. I realize it's early in the morning for a word like that, but it really isn't that complicated, and perhaps the best illustration of the idea comes from Harry Potter.

In the second book in the series, Harry and his friends have Transfiguration class, in which they are told to transform a pet into a teacup. Ron, whose wand is malfunctioning, waves his wand over his rat and comes up with a furry cup with a tail. But when they get it right, the rat turns into a teacup. It still is a rat, but it looks like a teacup. Transubstantiation is the opposite of that. The belief is that when certain words and gestures are performed over the bread and wine, it is transformed into the flesh and blood of Jesus. It still looks like bread and wine, but the substance has changed into the body and blood of Jesus.

About 500 years ago, during the Protestant Reformation, a few people had the courage to say "I don't believe that at all!" and another theology of the Eucharist was born, called *memorialism*. We eat the bread and drink from the cup because Jesus ate a Passover meal with his friends before he died, and because he told them to "do this in memory of me." And so we do. As Pastor John Buchanan of Fourth Presbyterian says, "It's just bread."

Anglicans, Episcopalians, are of course not content to choose between transubstantiation and memorialism, and of course Anglican theology is the one I find most difficult to explain. This theology is called *real presence*. When the bread and wine are brought to the table, blessed and broken, Jesus is really present in the bread and wine. It is still just bread and wine, but it has been transformed by the presence of Jesus. All of Jesus is present, body and spirit. How? It is a mystery we can't explain.

Of course none of this explains why the author of John has Jesus say, "Unless you eat my flesh and drink my blood, you cannot abide in me." Perhaps the author wants to shock us, get our attention. We have a tendency to think about Jesus and debate what we believe. We put Jesus, his words, and ideas into the rock tumbler of our minds.[4] We turn them around and around until they get smooth, and pretty, and harmless. But the author of John wants us to get real, fleshy. It is not about what we believe; it is about what we do. Maybe it isn't so important what happens to the bread and wine at this table, but what happens to us.[5]

You know when someone is really present. I know when I'm talking on the phone and someone is reading e-mail or surfing the net while talking to me. You know when someone is really listening, connecting. You know what it means to be really present. We have a phrase we use when something seems fake, unbelievable. "Get real!" we say.

What does it mean that Jesus is really present in the Eucharist? The best illustration I can think of again comes from Harry Potter. Remember the Polyjuice Potion? This is a potion that makes a person look and act like someone else. You mix the potion and add a hair from the person you want to turn into. You drink the potion, and then you have about an hour for whatever mischief you have planned, until it wears off and you look like yourself again. When we come to the altar rail and take the piece of bread and sip the wine, we don't come back looking like Jesus, but we are meant to act like him.

4   Image taken from Matt Fitzgerald in "Reflections on the Lectionary" *Christian Century*, August 11, 2009, pg. 21.

5   Like all my best lines, this one comes from my best friend, The Reverend Bridget Tierne, director of Advent House, Christ Church Cathedral, in New Orleans, Louisiana. She critiques and improves almost every sermon, and I hers, on Saturday afternoons.

"Unless you eat my flesh and drink my blood you cannot abide in me." Maybe it isn't so important what happens to the bread and wine at this table, but what happens to us at this table. We take the bread and wine, and we are transformed. We have the hands and feet, the heart and voice of Jesus. We are the real presence of Jesus in the world. When we eat this bread and drink this wine, Jesus abides in us, and we become Jesus to everyone we meet.

Peace Making

Isaiah 2:1-5

Just over nine hundred years ago Pope Urban the Second called for a crusade to capture Jerusalem from the Turks. There was no imminent threat, but property disputes between knights in Europe were erupting in violence, and the Pope thought warfare against an outside enemy might unite them. Over the next two hundred years, one hundred thousand men went to the Middle East, destroying cities and killing Muslims, Jews, and Christians.[6]

First Sunday of Advent

They shall beat their swords into plowshares,
and their spears into pruning hooks;
nation shall not lift up sword against nation,
neither shall they learn war any more.

This week in Annapolis, the headquarters of the Navel Academy, President Bush and Secretary of State Rice met with the leaders of Israel and the Palestinian Authority to resume Middle East peace talks. Prime Minister Olmert and President Abbas left the meeting after agreeing to meet every two weeks to forge a settlement. Can you see it? Can you imagine peace in Jerusalem, in Tehran, in Baghdad?

6   The Writer's Almanac with Garrison Keillor, Tuesday, November 27, 2007

> *They shall beat their swords into plowshares,*
> *and their spears into pruning hooks;*
> *nation shall not lift up sword against nation,*
> *neither shall they learn war any more.*

One night in a small Sri Lankan village a man was walking alone. Another man approached on a bicycle and threw a hand grenade, which exploded, injuring the man. The cyclist quickly rode away. Afraid for their lives, none of the neighbors came out of their houses. A member of the Nonviolent Peaceforce, an organization which trains and deploys peace workers, heard the explosion and ran to his aid. She took him to a hospital in time for his life to be saved. The next evening, the people of the village marched through the streets to celebrate the life saved and the courage of the Peace Worker. They committed to standing together and not succumbing to their fears.[7]

> *They shall beat their swords into plowshares,*
> *and their spears into pruning hooks;*
> *nation shall not lift up sword against nation,*
> *neither shall they learn war any more.*

As Christians it is tempting to use our belief in a savior to save us from acting: My life will be perfect when my knight in shining armor comes....This book says my kids will stop hitting each other when they get out of this phase....We will

---

7   http://www.nonviolentpeaceforce.org/participate

get out of this war if we just elect the right leaders....My road rage will end when I get a bigger car.

But Isaiah doesn't suggest that God will come and wipe away all the violence. He says *we* will do the work of making peace. Isaiah envisions the temple in Jerusalem as such an example to the world that people stream to the mountain to learn from God, "that he may teach us his ways and we may walk in his paths." God doesn't fix everything with the wave of a hand. He judges, arbitrates, meets out justice, and teaches the people the ways of peace—to plant, not kill; to harvest, not terrorize; to learn peace, not war.

> *They shall beat their swords into plowshares,*
> *and their spears into pruning hooks;*
> *nation shall not lift up sword against nation,*
> *neither shall they learn war any more.*

It is Advent, the time when we wait for the coming of the Prince of Peace. Except Isaiah doesn't want us to wait. Isaiah calls us out of our seats, out of our homes, out of church, off the computer, and into the world to start making peace. Because the opposite of violence is not doing nothing; the opposite of violence is not passivity. The opposite of violence is work, the hard work of making peace. It is putting on the armor of light, it is strength, the courage to face fear without weapons, to admit our failures, to stop threatening and start talking. We can do the work of making peace, whether we are teaching our children how to deal with bullies or facing the frustration of rush hour traffic; whether we are dealing with a person whose stupid mistake is screwing up our lives or recognizing Israel **and** Palestine as separate nations.

First, we have to admit reality: We responded to September 11 in fear....I insulted my brother-in-law....We allowed the Holocaust to happen....I drove like an idiot.... Second, we have to be willing to learn about the other, the stranger. It is no accident that the peace in Northern Ireland has held after peacemaking groups arranged for years the exchange of students—Protestant children living with Catholic families, Catholic students studying at Protestant schools. We need to know how much the war costs, in human lives and in dollars. Third, we have to treat peacemaking as a job to be learned, skills to acquire, work worth the cost. And finally, we have to commit ourselves to staying at the table. You can say you are never going to that person's house for Thanksgiving again, but it won't solve the argument. We need to tell our politicians to do what is right, insist on diplomacy first. Keep our kids talking. Visit our neighbors. Stay connected. Because the Prince of Peace isn't coming, until we let him come, until we make the peace we so desperately long for.

> *They shall beat their swords into plowshares,*
> *and their spears into pruning hooks;*
> *nation shall not lift up sword against nation,*
> *neither shall they learn war any more.*

Home Depot Greeter

Luke 21:25-36

I admit I am proud that I never shop on the weekend after Thanksgiving. I like to stay home and enjoy leftovers. However, I found myself on Saturday needing to do some Advent shopping. If my Sunday school class was going to make Advent wreaths, I needed supplies.

First Sunday of Advent

So there I was in Home Depot on Saturday afternoon looking for greens for our wreaths. As I entered the store I heard a voice from behind a mound of Christmas decorations singing "Here Comes Santa Claus" in a loud and somewhat out-of-tune voice. It was the Home Depot greeter, and I thought he was mocking the Muzak. So I said, "You'll be sick of that pretty soon."

"I know!" he said in a cheerful voice. "But it's the first day of Christmas shopping, and I love it!" He turned to the next customer coming into the store ("Welcome to Home Depot!") and handed out a sale flyer. Gosh, I felt like a curmudgeon!

The experience was kind of like walking into church on the first Sunday of Advent. There are beautiful greens by the front door, and wreaths inside. The Advent wreath is set up at the front of the church, and the vestments have finally changed from months of green to beautiful purple. And then Jesus walks down the aisle and says, "Watch out! The world is going to end!"

I've been preaching for seven years, so it is no surprise to me that I have to preach the end of the world on the first Sunday of Advent. But it still annoys me. I can't quite understand why we are reading about the end of the world. Can't we just have some Advent peace and quiet?

We are lucky this year, though. We are reading from Luke, and he's a little softer than the other gospel writers on the end-of-the-world stuff. As I read and sat with the gospel this week, I noticed something I hadn't seen before. Jesus' warnings seem to go from global to personal, and he gives a bit of advice about how to deal with the warnings.

First, Jesus talks about global disasters. "There will be signs in the sun and moon and stars" he says. These are natural disasters, part of living on this earth. These warnings sound a bit like the global warming warnings we hear now. Jesus says that when these natural disasters hit, we should lift up our heads and have hope. Some people react to the warnings about global warming by denying it, or not caring because they won't be alive when the world falls apart. On the other extreme, some people react with fear, paralyzed with the realization that everything they do harms the earth in some way. But Jesus suggests a different way, the way of hope. These warnings are an opportunity for us to do something—to change our ways and to take seriously the call given in our ancient story of creation. We are not owners of the earth, but stewards, charged with caring for the gift of creation. In the face of disaster, we can act with hope.

Next Jesus gets more local. He tells a simple story. "Look at the trees," he says. "You know when they blossom that summer is near." Read the signs he says, look at the realities. So, if kids have nothing to do after school but paint graffiti on our garages, there is something wrong at home, something needed in our schools. Read the signs. If there are people panhandling at Six Corners, then they need affordable housing, they need health care, and they need skills so that they can get jobs. Face the realities, says Jesus. But Jesus also says that when we see these signs, we know that God is near. Get close to the people who are suffering, because that is where you'll see God.

And then Jesus turns the heat on. "Get rid of these distractions," he says "dissipation and drunkenness and the worries of life." The harshest warnings are reserved for our personal life. My kids are tired of hearing me say it, but screen time sucks brain cells. Dissipation is entertainment, whatever distracts us from facing the realities of life. Alcohol does that too…drinking is an escape from the real stuff we need to face in our own lives. And what are the worries of life, especially at this time of year? Too much shopping! Jesus warns us about the alluring lies of advertizing: You aren't good enough, buy more! You don't love enough, spend! Whoever says religion is an escape has never listened to the readings for Advent. Jesus' words shine a bright light right on our personal stuff. And Jesus' advice? Be Alert! Get rid of the distractions so that you can face reality.

In fact we should all be more like the greeter at Home Depot. He wasn't thinking about the twenty-five days he'd be listening to the same song over and over again. He wasn't thinking about the pressures he'd face if sales didn't rise. He wasn't thinking about the day after Christmas when he'd be out of a job because the holiday rush was done. He was living in the moment, enjoying the music, connecting with the people who came his way—even the grumpy priest who didn't want to be shopping.

When there are global disasters, Jesus says, "lift up your heads, have hope!" When there are problems in our community Jesus says, "Look at the signs! God is near!" When our lives are crumbling, Jesus says, "Let go of your worries and be alert! Pay attention to the moment, so that you will be ready for Christ to come into your heart."

Phone Call

[My cell phone rings, I answer it.]
Hello?!

….

Yes, I'm just about to preach my sermon!

….

No, I'm not preaching that.

….

I told you, I have a plan. There are four Sundays in Advent and each one was about a gift we could give to the world. The first Sunday was about peacemaking, the second was about getting along with those who are different from us, and this Sunday is about healing.

….

No, I'm not preaching that. I'm not telling people to stop shopping. It's the week before Christmas! Half my congregation works in advertising and retail. I haven't finished my Christmas shopping. Where are you?

….

Standing in front of the Target at the HIP mall shouting "What would Jesus buy?" and "Save your soul, Stop Shopping!? Well, I'm standing in front of my congregation, and I'm supposed to be preaching a sermon.

....

Yes, I read the scriptures for today. That was my plan, to preach the Hebrew Scriptures during Advent. They are such beautiful poems from Isaiah, "The wilderness shall be glad and the desert shall blossom..."

....

Yes, I know the wilderness can't blossom if it's covered with a parking lot.

....

I read the gospel. It's about the time John the Baptist is in prison, and he sends his friends to ask Jesus if he is preaching God's word. Jesus says, "the blind see, the deaf hear, the dead are raised, what do you think?"

....

Yes, it does seem like there is a paragraph missing from this gospel! You can just tell that Jesus' disciples aren't too thrilled about having John's disciples hanging around. You can just hear them complaining to Jesus: Do you know who John the Baptist is? That crazy guy! He dresses weird and stands outside the city shouting at people about their sins. And you can almost imagine Jesus saying: Who did you expect to speak for God? A movie star in Gucci glasses? He's a prophet!

....

Look, I'm not going to preach "Stop Shopping!" This is a stressful time of year. People need to hear words of comfort.

We are doing prayers for healing today.

....

If we want healing we need to stop doing what's killing us? Are you blaming people for their illnesses?

....

I agree, when one out of four Americans are overweight it is not an individual problem. It's a disease our whole country has. We have too much, and we can't handle it.

....

I know some cancers are caused by environmental factors.

....

And, yes, if Chinese factories had the same standards as American factories we wouldn't be getting lead-tainted toys. If we paid Chinese workers living wages, outsourcing wouldn't look so good and there would be more jobs here.

....

Shopping is an addiction? Well I know that retail therapy isn't an accepted medical practice...

....

Look, I have people here who are grieving the loss of loved ones. You can't blame them for their grief.

....

Yes, we do put high expectations on this holiday. It's almost a crime to be unhappy this time of year. I can see how some people might avoid calling those they know are unhappy or suffering. We don't want anything to ruin our holiday mood.

….

What?! What's going on?

….

You see a security guard? And you are still shouting, "What would Jesus buy?"

….

No! Don't shout "Save your Soul: Stop Shopping!"

….

What did you expect? Call me when you get to jail.

[I hang up phone.]

That was my friend, JB. I sometimes call him for sermon advice. I don't know why. I never want to hear what he has to say.

So you heard it. If we want to be healed, we have to stop doing what's killing us.

Just remember, I didn't tell you to stop shopping. He did.

Have Politics Taken Over?

Matthew 22:15-22

Have politics taken over your life, too? It wasn't enough to have early primaries and the presidential race for two years. With three weeks left before the election, there is no place I can go to hide from the constant talk, polls, and ads. Now even

Twenty-third Sunday after Pentecost

Saturday Night Live has been invaded by real politicians. And what cruel joke does the church's lectionary choice have for us this morning? The religious lawyers asking Jesus, "Is it lawful to pay taxes to the emperor, or not?" Come on! They might as well have asked him, "Is it patriotic to pay taxes?" It must be patriotic! If giving your life for your country is the ultimate sacrifice, then giving your hard-earned money to the government must count for something. But it must be equally patriotic to complain about taxes and try to change how our money is spent.

"Is it lawful to pay taxes to the emperor, or not?" Jesus' famous answer is, "Give therefore to the emperor the things that are the emperor's and to God the things that are God's." But what belongs to the emperor and what belongs to God? On Wednesday I asked that question of our vestry, our church leaders. We began to carve up our week: "I work for the city, so forty plus hours go to the emperor." "Creativity belongs to

God." "My kids belong to God." "Most of my life belongs to the emperor."

What belongs to the emperor and what belongs to God? It is clear from the story that the Pharisees, the religious lawyers, and the Herodians (the Jewish puppet government) are trying to trap Jesus into saying something to get him in trouble so they can arrest him and get rid of him.

Why is the question such a dangerous one to answer? The Jews are a minority community under oppressive Roman rule. The Herodians are happy to do the dirty work for the Roman regime and skim off some of the profits while preserving their positions of power.[8] The Pharisees are more interested in making the Jewish people holy than questioning the Roman political power that enslaves the people.

But Jesus doesn't answer the question the way they had hoped. Jesus wants a different reality. He is called Son of David, the title for a Jewish king, and Son of God because he is both.

He wants everything—the Jewish people, the emperor, the empire, the whole world—to belong to God. The Pharisees and the Herodians don't arrest him because they, like us, think Jesus is telling us that it is okay to carve up our lives. This piece for the emperor, this piece for God. Jesus says it all belongs to God. "The Roman emperor thinks everything is

8   Wells, Sam. "Reflections on the Lectionary." The Christian Century, October 7, 2008.

his, Jesus insists that everything is God's. Nothing can be the emperor's without being first and always God's too."[9]

There was a bit of a crisis last month when the quilters were hanging their quilt show up here in the sanctuary. One of the ladies was desperate to find me.

"We are having an argument, a Roman Catholic and a Lutheran," she said. I got ready to dredge up what I learned in seminary. "We don't know if we can hang this quilt in the church. There are corsets on it!" (Corsets are old-fashioned ladies underwear, to you young people.) "Can we really hang it here? Should we hang it the basement?"

"It's fine!" I said. "The church was built in 1888, so it won't be the first time corsets have been in the church." And it is fine…everything belongs to God.

Then there was the discussion about the Mass with the Man in Black. Which Johnny Cash songs where "upstairs" songs, and which belonged at the party downstairs? "Give to the emperor the things that are the emperor's and to God the things that are God's".… Can we sing *Rusty Cage* or should we stick with *Personal Jesus*? Everything belongs to God. Or, as Ava wisely said while decorating for the party downstairs, "If you are afraid to tell God everything, what is the point of God?"

At Weight Watchers (while I cannot endorse a political

9   Ibid.

candidate from the pulpit, that is your product placement for this sermon)....At Weight Watchers I learned to write down everything I ate, every day. This is the most important thing you do in the program, because it forces you to see the food you eat without thinking, and the choices you make. You begin to make better choices.

I'm not going to eat that white bread, but I can put some cheese on my broccoli. I'll skip the store-bought coffee cake and have a slice of homemade banana bread instead. I won't snack all week, but I'll treat myself to chocolate on Sunday.

Maybe we should all go on the Empire Diet. Write down all the things you do in a week and then start circling. Extra hours at work...belong to God. A day of back pain...belongs to God. An hour with my kids in the car...belongs to God. A fight with my spouse...belongs to God. A good meal...belongs to God. Even an hour in church can belong to God.

You know the story of Jesus and the rich young man? This young man comes to Jesus. The man follows every commandment, goes to church, is good to everyone. "What more can I do to be saved?" he asks Jesus, sure to hear "you're practically perfect in every way," which is what everyone has always said to him.

But then Jesus says, "Go and sell everything you own and give the money to the poor." Sure, Jesus wants the poor to get a break, but more importantly, he wants to teach this young man that everything in his life belongs to God. We can hold nothing back.

Don't carve up your life between what belongs to the emperor and what belongs to God. It all belongs to God.

Metro Praise

1 Timothy 1:12-17

A new church—Metro Praise—is opening today in our neighborhood. It's located across from McNamara's on Irving Park Road, two blocks from St. John's. Two weeks ago I called the husband-and-wife pastors to welcome them to the

Sixteenth Sunday after Pentecost

neighborhood and invite them to coffee. So the other day I walked over to their church, which covers the entire second floor of a new storefront.

I must confess I was guilty of the sin of envy. I was jealous of their elevator, handicap accessible bathrooms, and AV equipment. Afterward, I showed them St. John's. We have everything they don't have—an historic building, stained glass, artwork, pews.

Then we started out for Starbucks. We were just out the door when the pastor asked me, "So what are your beliefs?" I wasn't quite prepared for the question, thinking we would get to know each other first, maybe share our experiences.

But luckily I went to seminary, and I was able to dredge up the "Chicago-Lambeth Quadrilateral." You can find it on page 876 of your prayer book. It outlines the four tenets which unite Anglicans/Episcopalians. They are that scripture is the revealed word of God, Baptism and Eucharist are the primary sacraments, the creeds are sufficient outlines of faith, and bishops are the order which unites us to the universal church. Metro Praise is a non-denominational, independent church. They have seven tenets of faith, including the Trinity and other basic Christian teachings we would agree on.

We hadn't yet placed our coffee order when she asked me, pointedly, if we practiced infant baptism. I knew we weren't going to pass muster on that. I tried to explain: we don't teach that baptism is an instant ticket to heaven; but that it is the beginning of the Christian journey, along which we renew our promises regularly. That didn't seem to ally her fears.

And then we got to the inevitable question, "Do you allow homosexuals to be pastors?" "Yes," I said.

"Don't you think they will go to hell if they don't confess and change their ways?" she asked.

"I don't know," I said. "I leave that for God to judge."

She quickly pulled out her iPhone to look up a scriptures passage to prove me wrong. I think she thought I was "ignorant in my unbelief" as Paul says in today's second reading. I have to admit I thought she was "ignorant in *her* unbelief." But I resisted the temptations to pull out a Bible verse or the historical context of first century Palestine to throw at her.

"Look," I said. "I knew when I called that there were a lot of things we wouldn't agree on. I just think it is important for Christians to work together on the things we can agree on."

Then I told her about Hands to Help, the Old Irving Park Community Food Pantry, and the Irving Park Community Clinic. She wanted to make sure there was no religious connection to these organizations, but she was interested in the clinic because many of their Bible college students do not have health insurance

The whole encounter left me uneasy. It was a microcosm of the dueling Florida pastors which has been going on nationally. I saw an interview on MSNBC with the Florida pastor who was going to burn the Quran. He said that God had told him not to do it. When asked at least three different times, he pledged that he would not now, and never would, burn the Quran.

MSNBC also interviewed another Florida pastor. He too was pastor of a non-denominational independent church. But this pastor put up a sign on the church lawn welcoming the Muslim Community Center across the way. He literally walked across the street to meet his Muslim neighbors. When the interviewer asked why he had done this, he said, "As I understand it, Jesus gave us two main commandments: 'love God and love your neighbor.' I don't see how burning the Quran falls under either of them." Of course, this pastor got a two-minute interview, while the other pastor had a ten-minute interview played over and over and over again.

What are we to make of all this? Paul gives us sound

advice in his letter to Timothy:[10]

"I am grateful to Christ Jesus our Lord, who has strengthened me, because he judged me faithful and appointed me to his service, even though I was formerly a blasphemer, a persecutor, and a man of violence."

Remember Paul? He was very sure about his religion, that he had it right. He was so sure, he persecuted Christians—that radical, new, dangerous sect. He oversaw Christians stoned to death. He writes, "But I received mercy because I had acted ignorantly in unbelief, and the grace of our Lord overflowed for me with the faith and love that are in Christ Jesus." That is what the other Florida pastor said. It is the faith and love of Christ that should flow out from Christians. Paul continues: "The saying is sure and worthy of full acceptance, that Christ Jesus came into the world to save sinners—*of whom I am the foremost.*" Too many Christians stop after the first half of the sentence, "Christ Jesus came into the world to save sinners," and then we start pointing our fingers at all the other people we think Jesus came to save. But it is the second half of the sentence in which Paul points the finger only *at himself*:

"But for that very reason I received mercy, so that in me, as the foremost, Jesus Christ might display the utmost patience, making me an example to those who would come

10   Actually, scholars tend to agree that this letter was not written by Paul, but by someone else in the style of Paul and using his name as a way to honor Paul as the author's teacher, a common practice in writings of the time.

to believe in him for eternal life. To the King of the ages, immortal, invisible, the only God, be honor and glory forever and ever. Amen."

Last Sunday my family and I were invited to an Iftar—the breaking of the Ramadan fast. We went with some Presbyterians, members of John's church, to an office building not unlike Metro Praise. We took an elevator up to a room set with a podium and tables and chairs, where members of the community greeted us. A professor and a member of the community lectured us on the meaning of Ramadan (demonstrating to our daughters that Islam can be just as boring as Christianity if someone stands up and talks about it too long). But then we went up to the prayer room. We stood on the carpet, which had lines indicating where we should stand so that we faced Mecca. The imam chanted and we bowed, and knelt, and put our foreheads to the ground, over and over again.

I don't know what my friends at Metro Praise would say, or what the Muslims thought, or even what God thought about me joining in the Muslim prayers. But I felt that I was humbling myself, bowing to my Savior Jesus Christ, who calls me to point fingers only at myself, and to let only faith and love flow out—the faith and love which has the power to transform the world.

Happy Father's Day!

Matthew 1:18-25

No, I haven't gotten my holidays confused. It just seems like we should recognize this one day, which only comes around once every three years, when we hear Joseph's side of the story. In Matthew's version of the birth of Jesus, the angel does not come to Mary, but to Joseph in a dream. Joseph discovers that Mary is pregnant, and he plans to save his

Fourth Sunday of Advent

reputation, and possibly save her from stoning, which was one of the punishments for adultery at the time. He decides he will end the engagement quietly. But the angel comes to him and tells him that this baby is special—that he will save his people from their sins. And so Joseph does the right thing and marries Mary. He deserves to be called a righteous man.

In *Christ the Lord, Out of Egypt,* Anne Rice imagines what it might have been like for eleven-year-old Jesus to discover the strange stories surrounding his birth. She traces the family's journey from Egypt, where they had fled to escape Herod, back to their hometown of Nazareth. Along the way family members let slip details of the story of Jesus's birth. When they arrive in Nazareth, the men of the family decide to go to the synagogue. When they walk in, the whole room goes silent, and everyone stares at Jesus. The rabbi walks slowly towards them. Joseph puts a protective arm around Jesus and says, "This is Jesus, my son." Eleven years haven't quieted the rumors about Mary, but the rabbi slowly nods and lets them in.

Did Joseph save Mary? No, it was God who was with her when she said "yes" to the angel. It was God who would have been with her regardless of what Joseph decided to do. But Joseph did the right thing. He decided to participate in God's salvation. Joseph deserves to be called a righteous man.

This week King Abdullah of Saudi Arabia pardoned the "Qatif girl." I don't know if you have been following her story. This young girl, nineteen years old, was engaged to be married. She wanted to get a photograph of herself from an ex-boyfriend. She was afraid he might use it against her to smear her reputation. So she agreed to meet him, which is against the law. They were caught by seven men who kidnapped and raped them both.

Rather than remain silent, the Qatif girl demanded justice. The seven men were given up to one thousand lashes and five years in prison. She was given ninety lashes for her "intention to do wrong." When her lawyer had the audacity to appeal her sentence, it was doubled. Due to international pressure King Abdullah pardoned her. The untold story is that her fiancé, even after what happened to her, married her and has stood beside her in her quest for justice.

King Abdullah didn't save the Qatif girl. Her husband didn't save her. It was God who was with her at that terrible moment. It was God who gave her the strength to demand justice. It is God who will be with her as she tries to put her life back together again. But King Abdullah and her husband did the right thing. They participated in God's justice. They deserve to be called righteous.

At the Hands to Help board meeting this week, we were presented with the situation of Sarah, a neighbor with a ten-year-old son. She recently had a baby she had to give up for adoption because she couldn't afford another child. She also lost her waitressing job. She couldn't pay her December rent, and her landlord was threatening to evict her. The good news is that she has a new waitressing job, starting in January. Hands to Help agreed to pay her December rent and part of her January rent so that she can keep her apartment. We didn't save Sarah and her son. It is God who will be with her as she struggles through this difficult time. But perhaps we have participated in God's justice and deserve to be called righteous.

Two days before Christmas is a wonderful time to recognize the fathers in our lives, and all those who do the right thing. It is a fine time to be reminded to listen to God's call, to listen to our dreams, and to dare to participate in God's justice, not in order to save others, but in order to save ourselves.

Discovering God

Jeremiah 31:1-6
Matthew 28:1-10

A six-year-old girl in Scotland decided to write a letter to God. Her parents, who are non-believers, were concerned that she get an answer to her question which was, "To God, How did you get invented?" Her father, being a good father,

Easter Sunday

sent the letter off. The Scottish Episcopal Church didn't answer, neither did the Presbyterians. The Scottish Catholics sent a "nice but theologically complex answer.[11]" But then the Archbishop of Canterbury, the head of the Anglican Communion wrote back. This is his letter.

> *Dear Lulu,*
> *Your dad has sent on your letter and asked if I have any answers. It's a difficult one! But I think God might reply a bit like this –*

> *'Dear Lulu – Nobody invented me – but lots of people discovered me and were quite surprised. They discovered me when they looked round at the*

---

11   http://blogs.telegraph.co.uk/news/damianthompson/100084843/a-six-year-old-girl-writes-a-letter-to-god-and-the-archbishop-of-canterbury-answers/

*world and thought it was really beautiful or really
mysterious and wondered where it came from. They
discovered me when they were very very quiet on
their own and felt a sort of peace and love they
hadn't expected.*

*Then they invented ideas about me – some of them
sensible and some of them not very sensible. From
time to time I sent them some hints – especially in
the life of Jesus – to help them get closer to what I'm
really like.*

*But there was nothing and nobody around before me to
invent me. Rather like somebody who writes a story
in a book, I started making up the story of the world
and eventually invented human beings like you who
could ask me awkward questions!'*

*And then he'd send you lots of love and sign off.
I know he doesn't usually write letters, so I have to do
the best I can on his behalf. Lots of love from me too.*

— Archbishop Rowan[12]

It is Easter Sunday morning, a morning to discover God
and be surprised. I think Archbishop Rowan is right about the

12   Ibid.

ways we can discover God.

If you want to discover God, look for something beautiful. As Jeremiah suggested, plant something with your hands, see it blossom and bear fruit. Do something creative that makes the world more beautiful.

If you want to discover God, ask the big, difficult questions, delve into the mysterious. The mystery that amazes me this morning is also from Jeremiah. He calls Israel a virgin! Can you believe that? A four thousand-year-old virgin! We know the stories, how Israelites were slaves in Egypt, how they were freed and wandered through the dessert, whining. How they invaded a land, committed genocide, were the victims of genocide. Some virgin! That is a mystery, how God can know and love and forgive us, no matter what. We can be virgins again.

Rowan says if you want to discover God be very quiet, and feel peace and love you hadn't expected. Take time with a memory; let it be healed.

There are many, many ways to discover God. I think there is one that Rowan doesn't mention, and that is right here, in community. This is why I became a priest; so that every Sunday I could discover God sitting in these pews, people praying, singing, crying, squirming. It is in community that I discover God.

The story of the cross and tomb reminds us that even in the midst of death and despair, God is to be found; God goes with us wherever we are.

And the story of the women going to the tomb reminds us that God is not where you last left off: He is not here! He has been raised!

Have you discovered God? This is the day! This is the day to discover God, if you never have, or if you have forgotten the beautiful, mysterious love and peace of God. Discover God. Be surprised.

About St. John's Episcopal Church

The parish of St. John's Episcopal Church began as a small Sunday School in 1883 in Old Irving Park. A neighborhood congregation committed to worship and service, St. John's is a diverse group of people of all ages, races, abilities, and sexual orientation.

Throughout its history, St. John's has been involved in reaching out to the community and has been most known for a free home-cooked Thanksgiving meal served every year since the 1980s.

Currently, the community of St. John's is involved in a partnership with the Diocese of Southeast Mexico, Hands to Help Ministries, which serves the local homeless population, and is the drop-off site for Genesis Growers, a Community Supported Agriculture organic farm.

The church is located on Chicago's northwest side. Additional information may be obtained on the St. John's website: *www.stjohnschicago.com*

About the author

Kara Wagner Sherer (b. 1969) grew up in Marshall, Minnesota. Her first piece of writing, at age five, was a Christmas pageant, performed in the laundry room of her apartment building. She was Mary, of course.

Kara preached for the first time at age 17 at St. James Episcopal Church in Marshall on the Sunday after Easter. The people in her parish encouraged her to become a priest, but her plans were to be an English teacher. She preached again as a senior at St. Olaf College in Northfield, Minnesota, again ignoring advice to pursue the ministry.

Kara taught third and fifth grades for six years. After marrying her husband John and moving to New York City, she found herself living across from General Theological Seminary. She got the hint. After graduating from Seabury-Western Theological Seminary in Evanston, Illinois, she was ordained a priest in 2003.

She served as the Assistant Rector at St. Paul & the Redeemer in Chicago for two years, and was called to be Rector of St. John's Episcopal Church in 2005. She and her husband John, a Director of Music, have two daughters, Madeleine and Carlisle.